*Forgi*

Psalms 27:13

Charlotte

*Forgive and Remember*

# *Forgive and Remember*

## *A Journey from Forgiven to Forgiveness*

### By

### Charlotte A. Fortier

2013

*Forgive and Remember*

Book Title: Forgive and Remember, A Journey from Forgiven to Forgiveness

Author Name: Charlotte A. Fortier

Copyright © Charlotte A. Fortier

Printed in the United States of America

Book Design by Charlotte A. Fortier

First Edition: September, 2013

ISBN-13: 978-1481025966

ISBN-10: 1481025961

*Forgive and Remember*

## Dedications

I dedicate this book to God, the Father, God, the Son, and God, the Holy Spirit. They proved to me beyond doubt, that, *"the word of God is living and powerful, and sharper than any two-edged sword, piercing even to the division of soul and spirit, and of joints and marrow, and is a discerner of the thoughts and intents of the heart. "*(Hebrews 4:12 NKJV)

## Special Thanks

To my husband, Herb, whose love for me, and faith in me, bolstered my courage to write. His technical assistance with computers, etc., saved this book from being only a dream.

To my best friend, Charlotte Callahan, who listened, cried, laughed, prayed, and believed with me, that someday I would publish what God had done in me and for me.

To Jody Raikowski, who heard my story, opened a door, and helped me to complete this journey.

## *Forgive and Remember*

To my 'divine connection," Sharon Cook, who gave her time, and talents to help me realize my dream, and became my friend.

To Karen, my Lakeside friend, and to Suzy Q (Susan Stewart), who critiqued my book, invested their time, blessed my soul, and gave me a glimpse of what words can do to change a heart.

To all my family and friends, who throughout my life, gave me encouragement and support. My life is a reflection of these wonderful people.

# TABLE OF CONTENTS

*Forgive and Remember*

# INTRODUCTION

The Bible is a history book. It contains real life stories of men and women who have learned to know the Living God. Many have struggled to understand the Bible, and have concluded it is no longer relevant, and difficult to understand.

I have written this book, as my own testimony, to the power that is in the Word of God, and its ability, when given time and dedication, to change even the most hardened heart.

An entire nation called Israel witnessed the awesome strength and majesty of God, as He transformed them from a slave nation, to a ruling nation. This same God, humbled Himself, came in the likeness of human flesh to die on a cross in order that one day I could also witness the transformation He would make in me.

I do not write this as a Biblical scholar, nor as one who holds this world's credentials. I write as a living witness, who was once dead in her sins, and yet, received new life through faith in Christ Jesus.

The journeys of old became my journey of the present. The same God Who led the Israelites to their Promised Land, led me to my freedom. I know that Jesus is the same yesterday, today, and forever. May you discover new hope and courage as you witness my journey, which took place over fourteen years ago, and yet the truths revealed to me are as fresh as the day God revealed them to me.

*Forgive and Remember*

*Forgive and Remember*

# GOD'S LEADING

*I may forgive you, but I will never forget!*

These words have held more people in bondage than they have helped to set free. Why is this true? An offense affects the mind, will and emotions of a person. Since all three parts are affected, then all three parts need restoration.

True forgiveness seems impossible to us. Even when we hear or read of how Jesus forgave, deep in our hearts we wonder if it is true. Our souls can hold onto the words and actions of people forever because the mind is such a marvelous instrument of memory. Are there moments when you relive hurtful moments even though it is years later? Do you feel condemned when you have tried to forgive and failed?

I have been there. I was inspired to write this book in the desire to help others walk in victory over persecutions, past hurts, and destructive words that still reside in their souls, even though they have tried in every way possible to forgive the person or persons who have wounded them.

God's Word offers the tools to have a life that says, "I've forgiven and I remember." I am neither a trained psychiatrist nor a medical professional, but I have come to know Jehovah-Rapha, the God Who heals and restores the soul. Psalms 23 is a favorite scripture for many, but it was when the Holy Spirit quickened verse 3 to me, *"He restores my soul,"* that I began to understand that my salvation was so much more than just waiting to go to heaven.

The Hebrew word for "restore" means to return, to restore to a former condition, to make whole, to repair, and that is precisely what the Lord began to reveal to me through the act of "forgive and remember." His name is not Jehovah-Band-Aid. He is the God, Whose healing powers, has never changed (Hebrews 13:8).

*Jesus Christ is the same, yesterday, today, and forever.*

If you are human, then you have suffered abuse or hurt at some point in your life. Over time, these abuses can become layers of hurt, like the layers of an onion, or like scar tissue that builds up after a cut or surgery. Sometimes we can go on and put it all behind us until another incident opens that scar, and in an instant of time, we are hearing those voices again, feeling the anger, the shame, the humiliation of that moment, and we have to expend the time and energy just to get past it again.

Instead of "forgive and remember", I used "forgive and forget" many times in my life, not because I truly forgave, but I wanted to find some way to have the upper hand. In this book, I share how God taught me to "forgive and remember." This godly secret will cleanse hurtful memories and emotions, and will help you move into freedom. God will replace the memories you carry now with ones that will transform you by His grace and mercy. If you will read and agree to do what I suggest later in this book, have patience, and make a commitment, you can be free. I have used this godly method many times, and it has never failed me.

Hebrews 13:5b-6 gives us God's Promise:

*"I will never leave you nor forsake you," so we may boldly say: "The Lord is my Helper; I will not fear. What can man do to me?"*

In the next chapter, I relate a personal story for illustration purposes, and not to condemn anyone in the telling of it, for I know now who the real enemy of my life is, and it is NOT people! In John 10:10, Jesus pulled back the curtain on that behind-the-scenes destroyer:

*"The thief does not come except to steal, and to kill, and to destroy. I have come that they may have life, and that they may have it more abundantly."*

The life spoken of here is the God-kind of life. It is an overcoming life. Satan takes life. In Mark 4:16-19, as Jesus taught by the sea to the multitude, He revealed what causes the soul of a person to fail and stumble. He points the finger directly at Satan, and the lack of knowledge that most of us operate in regarding his tactics and assaults.

*And in the same way the ones sown upon stony ground are those who, when they hear the Word, at once receive and accept and welcome it with joy; And they have no* **real root in themselves***, and so they* <u>*endure for a little while*</u>*; then when* **trouble or persecution** *arises on account of the Word, they immediately are offended (become displeased, indignant, resentful) and they stumble and fall away. And the ones sown among the thorns are others who hear the Word; Then* **the cares and anxieties of the**

8

*world and distractions of the age, and the pleasure and delight and false glamour and deceitfulness of riches, and the craving and passionate desire for other things creep in and choke and suffocate the Word, and it becomes fruitless.*

Look very carefully at the above scripture. Consider what it means to have a *root* in your heart. In the natural world we live in, the root of any vegetation serves a vital purpose. It absorbs water and nutrients, stores them, anchors the plant body to the ground, and aids in its reproduction. I attempt a garden every year, and have learned how important it is to have the proper soil for vegetables to thrive. Whether I plant seeds, or live plants, the preparation of the soil is imperative for success.

This parable is bringing a comparison between a natural and a spiritual condition. It reveals the problems of all human hearts, and gives the solution that will correct that particular condition. If you are reading this book, and do not yet have a personal relationship with Jesus Christ, then, I invite you to go to the back of this book for instruction on how to receive Him into your heart.

### *Forgive and Remember*

I write this as a Christian, whose life was a very "thorny" one at that time. I loved God, His Word, and wanted to be a witness of His love to others. Because I had no *real root in my heart*, I opened wide the door for the enemy to come against my mind. I was full of care and anxiety. The little knowledge I possessed of God's Word, did not find a healthy, growing environment in my heart. I did not recognize at the time that Satan was using past hurts against me, accusing others to me, and continually laying a path of destruction for my future, which I willingly followed. I did not understand how he craftily used my own ignorance of God's Word to keep me emotionally in chains.

Stay with me now as God reveals the next step to "forgive and remember." Every journey to freedom begins with one step. You will be encouraged!

*Forgive and Remember*

*Forgive and Remember*

# FACING THE JORDAN

In the early 1990s, I was working at a financial institution, helping my husband start a ministry, a mother of two young daughters, and wanting desperately to quit my job. In other words, I was already living in a continual state of turmoil and unrest that began to pave the way toward the events that were to take place. I held positions of authority both at work and at church, but answered to a supervisor on my job, which I slowly began, over the years, to treat with less and less respect.

The stressful relationship we had was due to my attitude, pure and simple. Yes, this person had faults, and at that time, I capitalized verbally on them, which was very unkind and thoughtless. Let me also say that this person did not seek to make my life miserable. The misery in my heart before becoming her employee. It found a way to manifest as I "took" offense, and lived in it. Before I go further with this, I need to insert a portion of my past to bring greater clarity to the diseased root that brought forth the bitter fruit in my heart.

I came from a very abusive home. The display of severe authority that we were under the heel of as children, filled me with anger and established emotional scar tissue in me that broke open repeatedly in my relationships with people. Did I understand that then? No. All I knew was that the person I was working under, who demanded my respect, did not deserve it according to my constant critique of her work habits. Of course, the standard I held her to was my own, and *I* always came out the one who was right.

My father was handsome, charming, and charismatic to complete strangers; to me, he was a frightening man, and not a father. A professional psychiatrist would possibly describe him as schizophrenic. I believe there was some form of demonic oppression, due to his irrational behavior, coupled with violent outbursts of anger.

. My father suffered abuse as a child, and lived most of his life abusing. He left a trail of heartache, fear, and emotional pain in the hearts of those who loved him. The love that he gave was broken and selfish, and it damaged my soul. He was married five times, and all of his relationships ended in pain and sorrow due to his inability, and darkness of soul, to create a healthy family. We all suffered.

It is difficult to put in black and white, the evil deeds of someone who is supposed to be your protector. He was cruel when it came to the treatment of his family. After he divorced my mother, he delighted in finding ways to torment her. He manipulated the legal process in gaining custody of my three siblings and me. On certain weekends, he would grant permission for our mother to take us to her home. We would pack our bags, go out to meet her, and as we would reach for the car door, he would stop us. We dared not cry as we followed him back into the house.

I do not want to highlight my fathers' sins, as though they were the sum total of his life. He had many wonderful qualities, but they were not allowed to come to the forefront and therefore, we only knew the part of him that caused fear.

Poverty, fear, and shame were the legacies he left for us, and those roots sink deeply into a child's memory. But, praise God, when I became born again, I received a Father Who did not give me a spirit of fear, but one of power, love and a sound mind (2 Timothy 1:7).

In 1974, I became pregnant with my first beautiful daughter. I called my father to share this excitement with him. When Daddy answered the phone, I burst out with, "Daddy, I'm going to have a baby!" His reply was, "Oh, my back has been hurting lately." I expressed my sympathy and hung up. He died before my child was born; one more layer of scar tissue.

I relate this story because this one person's words and actions made an indelible impression upon me as a child, a teenager, a wife, and mother. Those wounds colored my attitude toward anyone who I saw as unjust, unfair, or uncaring. Several years later, as I was learning the true worship of God, He opened my heart to feel the unconditional love He had for my father. His grace brought understanding to my mind as to how God could love the sinner yet hate the sin. There are those who would say that

### *Forgive and Remember*

God "allowed" this in my life to help mold me into the woman I am still becoming. This is not Biblically true, though. God spoke to my heart that day and told me that the plan for my father was Psalms 1:

*Blessed is the man*
*who walks not in the counsel of the wicked,*
*nor stands in the way of sinners,*
*nor sits in the seat of scoffers;*
*but his delight is in the law of the LORD,*
*and on his law he meditates day and night.*
*He is like a tree planted by streams of water*
*that yields its fruit in its season,*
*and its leaf does not wither.*
*In all that he does, he prospers.*
*The wicked are not so,*
*but are like chaff that the wind drives away.*
*Therefore the wicked will not stand in the judgment,*
*nor sinners in the congregation of the righteous;*
*for the LORD knows the way of the righteous,*
*but the way of the wicked will perish.*

Because God gave my father a free will, he made the choice to walk in the way of the flesh and not the Spirit. By making these choices, he subjected all his relationships to the consequences of his own sin. We will eventually do the very same to our families if we do not understand the will of God that is set forth in His Word. Jesus, God's Son, was sent *to destroy the works of the devil* (I John 3:8). Jesus came to save, to restore, and to bring the blessing of wholeness back to shattered lives.

Joyce Landorf, author of *Irregular People,* used a phrase describing certain personalities as "irregular." She speaks of her own mother who never was able to enter into Joyce's life on an emotional basis, and left deep wounds in her soul. Joyce would begin a conversation with her mother, who would trail off into something completely different as though Joyce had never spoken.

Now my supervisor at work exuded that same kind of irregularity. This person was a three-piece suit that emanated an emotional distance, and an inability to enter into the personal lives of those who worked for her. Many times, she passed her duties onto our already overloaded schedules, simply because she did not want to handle it. Being in a minor role of authority, I found myself in the middle of many conflicts that erupted due to the ineffectiveness of this superior. Sarcasm and criticism are not my goals in this description of her. This was my perception of her at this particular point of my life.

I would awaken each morning dreading to go to work. Dread produced apprehension, and an unceasing sense of inferiority that I lived with every day. My mindset at that time was in constant turmoil. I hated my job, but like most couples in ministry, it helped to pay our bills while we trusted the Lord for full separation into ministry.

Oh, I wasted so much time living in self-pity, anger, and resentment in those days! Let me pause here and encourage those who are struggling with a difficult situation to learn how to praise God. What I mean by that phrase is turn to God's Word on a daily basis, and find scriptures that reveal His goodness, mercy and grace. Learn to focus your mind upon the One Who knows the plan.

*For I know the plans I have for you, declares the LORD, plans for welfare and not for evil, to give you a future and a hope.* Jeremiah 29:11

God has a future for you!

The disrespect that ruled in my heart during those days manifested itself in open criticism toward my supervisor, and **I** gladly shared that poison with those I supervised. In addition, I frequently confronted her. Whenever I had to confer with her, I would find ways to prove I was better at my job than she was. Pride is such an evil sin. I could, or should I say I would, not find any good in her—I just flat refused! **I** wanted recognition. **I** wanted acknowledgement. **I** wanted to be right!! Yet, deep in my soul, I knew just how very wrong I was; how very hypocritical I was.

I had been a Christian for years. I sang on the praise team and was a pastor's wife, a teacher of God's Word, a mother of two young daughters, and an emotional Mt. Saint Helens! It didn't take much to make me spew ash and smoke!!

I would praise the Lord on Sundays, and grit my teeth on Mondays just to get into my car and go to work. My soul was an emotional roller coaster ride from hell, and I did not know how to get off.

*Forgive and Remember*

*Forgive and Remember*

# PICKING UP THE STONES

The personal condemnation and dissatisfaction with my actions and attitudes was growing, and conviction over my anemic Christian lifestyle was eating me up from the inside out. If anyone wanted to know that there was a living, loving Savior, he would have had to look at someone other than me, because Jesus was definitely not Lord of my life during that time.

I knew **I** had to change. Even in that dawning knowledge, I wanted someone else to take the blame. It happened in the Garden of Eden, and still happens today.

Don't shut the book on me now! We have all been in that place of blaming someone else for the misery we are living in. We do not have to stay in misery. God does not approve of anyone inflicting pain or suffering on us, and what has or is being done to us is not right, for our restoration to begin and bring us to victory, we have to move out of a victim mentality. A victim is one who is injured, destroyed, or sacrificed under any of various conditions. Victim mentality is a personality trait in which a person tends to regard him or herself as a victim of negative actions of others, and to think, speak, and act as if that were the case—even in the absence of clear evidence.

You see, I "thought" my supervisor was my problem! Satan always offers a victim for the expression of our sin. As long as he can keep us looking outward towards others, he knows that this will be the stumbling block that will hinder us from repenting and receiving inward restoration from God.

Romans 1:16 says, *The Gospel is the power of God, unto salvation.* The word salvation comes from the Hebrew word *niphal*: "deliverance, help, safety, welfare, and prosperity." When you read God's Word on a continual basis, believe me, you will experience all of the above. *God's Word is alive and powerful and sharper than any two-edged sword* (Hebrews 4:12). As I continued to study the Bible, each scripture became a living stone that created a pathway to fully understanding the will of God. *The entrance of God's Word brings light* (Psalms 119:30) and that light is holy and pure, penetrating into your very soul *(mind, will and emotions).*

## *Forgive and Remember*

I had to change. I needed to change. What I wanted was a permanent − Jesus kind of change — that would show victory in my life rather than the constant defeat I lived in.

While reading one day, Matthew 18:35 spoke to my heart:

*So also, My heavenly Father will deal with every one of you if you do not freely forgive your brother **from your heart** his offenses.* (Emphasis mine).

I had taken offense at the actions and words of someone, and daily it became larger, and filled with color! You may be thinking that this does not seem like such a big deal compared to the suffering that some have been through. You are right! This incident was not THE big deal. Before this, many little deals had accumulated over the years. It is like the earth that surrounds a fault line. Pressure builds up, the plates of that fault line crash together, and then comes the earthquake.

The phrase, *from the heart*, captured my attention. We can forgive mentally, knowing this is what we should do. However, sincere forgiveness, from the heart involves mind, will and emotions. It is a total commitment to that act which sets one free in the realm of the soul. This is how I truly wanted to live; free from destructive emotions.

I cried out to God asking Him to forgive me and to help me forgive my supervisor from the heart. I did not understand how great the blessing was going to be in my life. God sees so much more than we do, and asks that we learn to trust Him.

He spoke to me, and told me to write down these words, *"I want you to forgive and remember, not forgive and forget."* I had never heard a statement like this before, and God would more than amaze me in what He had planned.

When I tell someone that I may forgive his or her words or actions, but I will never forget the offense, I am holding onto that offense in my heart, while patting myself on the back as though I have accomplished some noble deed. This kind of forgiveness is only a half act. The God kind of forgiveness is a full action, a sincere flow of His grace in the heart, which loves the sinner above the sin. This leaves no open wound or scar tissue that may rip open again in the future. When we forgive, it is not to exalt ourselves above that person or to seek to gain some upper hand. It is to become a channel of God's love that is released upon the offender.

I John 4:16-18 says *that perfect loves casts out fear.* When we are infused with the perfect (mature) love of God, we will not be afraid of forgiving the way He does. The unlovely, undeserving person, who became a tool of Satan to harm us, now becomes the object that God's grace focuses on.

Ephesians 2:1 clearly states, *and you He made alive, when you were dead (slain) by (your) trespasses and sins.* In this, we see the all-encompassing love of God toward the vilest offender. God does not excuse sin. God paid for sin through the sacrifice of His own Son. He offered mercy to all who would receive it; not based on their deserving it, but giving freely and generously to a world that was unable to save itself.

God gave us His perfect love in our born again spirits. This love came with God's ability to see others in the light of His grace. God looked upon us before we knew Him; while we were dead in our trespasses, *Christ died for us.* (Romans 5:8).

Therefore, I wrote in my journal what the Lord commanded me to, not knowing how this was going to work. The Holy Spirit influenced me to read the Book of Joshua, chapters 3 and 4. I read the amazing account of God leading His people from the slave lands of Egypt, across the River Jordan, to the land He had prepared for them, and I began to see how God was going to deliver me from a life of anger, condemnation, and bondage.

God gave Joshua explicit instructions in these chapters as to the protocol of the journey through the Jordan. First, the Levitical priests were to carry the Ark of the Covenant before the people. David, the king of Israel, wrote in Psalms 119:39, *Your Word is the lamp unto my feet and the light unto my path.* The Ark of the Covenant represented the spoken Word of God, because it held the commandments given to Moses on Mount Sinai.

Secondly, the people were to sanctify themselves, which is a holy preparation of the heart to follow the authority of God. God desires to show Himself strong on behalf of His people, and we must be willing to respond to God's plan. Romans 12:2 commands us to *present ourselves as a living sacrifice.* When we respond in obedience, God promises that *we will prove for ourselves what is His good, acceptable, and perfect will.* The part of your soul that is so very important for you to understand is your "will." The power to choose is what Satan wants to control. Watchman Nee, author of *The Spiritual Man*, tells how Satan came after the will of Eve through a physical need and her curiosity. Choice is what brought Adam and Eve to disobey. Choice brings us either to victory or defeat.

God desires that we see His wonders today in our lives just as the Israelites did. We have to learn how to cooperate with God, resist disobedience to His Word, and prepare our own hearts to follow Him. This time of preparation is crucial. We must discipline ourselves to read God's Word until it changes our very way of thinking and acting.

Remember that the born again child of God HAS received the life of God. He loves us so much that He gave ALL that He is, because we were dead in our sins, unable to help ourselves. This life brings new ideals and new attitudes that transform the person from the inside out. Israel did not have that blessing, for they were under a different covenant than the believer is today.

The Lord further encouraged Joshua that He would be with him, and those anointed words were spoken over the Israelites. Jesus promised the New Testament believer that He would send Someone to be with us forever; the Mighty Holy Spirit, Who would indwell the spirit of the born again one, never to depart. In John 14:16 we read that the Third Person of the Godhead, the Holy Spirit will *remain with you forever!* He comes with comfort, help, counsel, wisdom and strength from God.

When the soles of the priest's feet touched the waters of Jordan, the flowing river stopped and the waters coming down from above stood in a heap at Adam, the city that is beside Zarethan. The waters stood still! How powerful is the anointing of God in the life of the obedient?! The people then began to pass over. Folks, this did not take place in just a couple of hours. Millions of people walked across on dry ground. Have you ever been at a large arena or gathering of people, and when it was time to leave, you knew that the wait would be long due to traffic? Imagine the priests standing there for hours, bearing the Ark of the

Covenant before them! God wanted the Israelites to see the power of His Word. God wants YOU to see this in your life.

After the people had passed, the Lord spoke once again to Joshua, commanding him to take twelve stones from the midst of the Jordan, from **the very place where the priest's feet had stood**, and carry them over, to lay them down in the place where they were to lodge that night.

These stones, which represented the twelve tribes, became the sign to all the generations of the Israelites, of the guidance, love, and wonders that God had performed for them. The human mind has a tendency to forget the goodness of God after a crisis has passed, but when a memorial has been erected for a certain event, its continual presence refreshes the mind, of the wonderful details of that moment in history.

The question now arises as to what this has to do with learning how to "forgive and remember." This particular passage of Israel's history taught me the right way to use my memory. Our minds are wonderful creations that receive data, store it for future use, and recall it when needed. It also holds a record of every event of the human life, whether for good or for evil. When we have been loved, surprised, abused, traumatized, or affected in any way, what we have experienced is vividly recorded, along with all the emotion we felt. Most people can tell you in astonishing detail an event that altered their life from years ago, as though it took place today.

The Israelites had lived as a slave nation for hundreds of years. This lifestyle was rooted in their conscience. Enslavement renders a human to the lowest point possible in order to control their every thought and action. I have been a physical slave to pain, and I have lived enslaved to emotions of hatred and anger due to the ungodly actions of others. I have tramped the mud pits of self-pity and depression, due to time spent with my thoughts—captive and tormented by past offenses and abuses. You may have experienced this, also, and like me, have longed for real freedom and peace of mind.

I assure you that your journey to freedom is planned. The same God Who reached down and saved an entire nation of slaves, is the same God Who came to this earth in human form to pay the eternal price for you.

The Israelites encountered amazing occurrences along their journey, and every time they told their children the story of this crossing, and looked at those memorial stones, the emotions of fear turned to gladness as they **remembered** and spoke of God's delivering power.

There was no magical power in those particular stones, so don't run out looking for rocks!! The power came in **remembering** what God had performed for them. God's grace began to heal their memories by putting before them an object that reminded them of freedom.

They OBEYED the instruction of the Lord and entered their Promised Land. God changed them from a slave nation to a praise nation, just as He has promised to do for the man or woman *who will trust in the Lord with all their hearts, lean not unto their own understanding, but in all their ways acknowledge Him. He will then make plain and straight the path before them.* (Proverbs 3:5-6)

He was training them in the process, described in Romans 12:1-2, called the *renewing of the mind*. A renewed mind is one that receives new ideals, new attitudes, and has the godly wisdom to recognize the intent of a thought as it presents itself. This comes from a personal relationship with Jesus Christ.

At the beginning of this book, I quoted a saying that you may have thought or said sometime in your life: *I may forgive you but I will never forget.* This is a commonly accepted, worldly philosophy. It does not work. Memories and emotions are linked together.

God wants to transform those hurtful memories, and replace damaging emotions with ones that give you the experience of hope, joy, and peace. He wants to do an eternal exchange in your mind. He desires to replace the damage done to your soul, with new images of His goodness. You can learn to *forgive and remember*, just as I have.

One of my favorite scriptures that came alive to me was Psalms 23:4:

*Yes, though I "walk through" the (deep, sunless) valley of the shadow of death, I will fear or dread no evil; for You are with me; Your rod (to protect) and Your staff (to guide), they comfort me.*

## *Forgive and Remember*

Note: the two words *walk through.* God cares about the **details** encoded in your mind. If I am driving through a valley, I may get glimpses of the area I am passing through, but I am missing the details. Should I get out and walk that same area, I could then tell you in vivid detail the look of the stones, the colors of the trees, the outside temperature, etc. When I am on a journey, as important as learning how forgive sincerely, I must be aware of every tactic Satan may use to stop my progress. I must learn to be on guard with my emotions as details are encoded there, also.

The past memories that have grieved our souls (mind, will and emotions), are filled with sights, sounds, smells and feelings. God wants us to have the experience of *walking through* those experiences with Him, with confidence, knowing we are on our way to true liberation.

What is so glorious about this verse is that He is *with* us on this walk, just as He was with the nation of Israel. Our gracious and noble High Priest, the Lord Jesus Christ, Who walked this earth as a Man, has come to live IN us, to share this journey with us, to go over the details of our lives, cleansing, healing, and *restoring our souls* (Psalms 23:3).

## *Forgive and Remember*

I mentioned earlier that the Lord instructed me to write down the words...*I want you to forgive and remember, not forgive and forget!* Therefore, I purchased a journal, wrote down this precious phrase, not understanding at that point how this was going to unfold. As the Israelites prepared to obey God before their journey, so was I beginning the preparation of my heart.

In this journal, I was specifically told to record the date and time that I was to begin my journey to *sincerely forgive from the heart.* Next, I wrote a mission statement. It was... *On this date and time, I choose to forgive* (the name of the person). *Every time I look at this journal entry, I will REMEMBER that I made the choice to forgive, and I will not turn from this decision. This is my memorial stone to freedom. I will honor my word to God.*

God then instructed me to write down ALL the offenses that I had kept in my heart about my supervisor. He then told me to declare verbally my choice to forgive all of them. He then told me to take this paper outside, burn it, and again declare that this person was forgiven in my heart, and that I would honor God by *remembering* this decision before Him.

## *Forgive and Remember*

Sounds spiritual, huh? Listen, the real test of my decision came as I had to *walk through* each day living *outwardly* what the Lord had revealed to me *inwardly.*

Day after day as I encountered this person, I had to go to that journal and look at my decision to forgive. Why? Because her face and voice were a constant reminder of the various offenses. The work bathroom became a haven I retreated to, in order to keep control of my emotions. I worked at remembering the choice to forgive rather than focusing on supervisor's offenses. Many opportunities arose to add boulders to the mountain of hurt, but when I purposed to remember my commitment to *forgive*; one more pebble would come off that mountain.

How marvelous are the ways of God?!

There were many times when the enemy would accuse me and try to make me feel that all of this was useless. Though I failed at times, I would grab my journal, go over my decision and exalt God's Word over my emotions. When God reveals a truth to you, it is up to you to fight to hang onto that vision in spite of everything that comes against you.

As time passed, the feelings of dread and anger about going to work lessened. I kept practicing and remembering my decision, and would go back again and again to that journal. I read those words aloud repeatedly, because of the emotional battle surrounding this person.

After several months, my yearly work review was at hand. In the past, they were not very happy events. This year, as I stepped into my supervisor's office, it was with a new sense of peace.

She looked at me as I sat down and said, "Charlotte, what has happened to you?" I shook my head and asked what she meant. She continued by saying, "Our relationship has been very hard, you know, but in the past few months I have seen a real change come over you, and I just want to know what has happened."

I began to share with her the story you have read, and she began to cry. I felt an overwhelming desire to ask for her forgiveness! Months ago, I felt she owed me an apology for even breathing in the same room I was in, and now I wanted her forgiveness. I apologized for all the hurt I had caused, and the disrespect I had shown. She stood up, walked over to me and hugged me with tears in her eyes.

This woman was NOT a hugger and it really surprised me. After she sat down, she proceeded to tell me that after having witnessed the change in my attitude, that not only was she going to give me a raise, but a new job title that would open a new pay scale for me. I started crying. Not only had the Lord healed my soul, but also, He had brought something about that I had not expected.

As I sat there, the sense of being pleasing to God came over me. Jesus said that He came not to do His will but the will of the Father. He embraced the cruel cross, forgiving His enemies, and set the example of *forgive and remember.* In Hebrews 8:12 the precious words, *"I will forgive their wickedness and remember their sins no more,"* are the beacon lights that point the way for us to follow Him.

The months of believing and obeying God had borne its righteous fruit. I was a changed woman. I was no longer under the heavy load of guilt and condemnation. Jesus had taught me His way of forgiving, and I received a truth that would become an integral part of my life from that moment on.

## *Forgive and Remember*

Hebrews 4:16 speaks of *having boldness to enter the throne room of grace and mercy.* Our Savior does not condemn us for our failures or sins, because He became sin for us that we could receive the unconditional love of God. 1 John 1:9 bolsters our faith as we read that *if we confess our sins, He is faithful and just to forgive us of all our trespasses and continually cleanse us from ALL unrighteousness, (*emphasis mine).

I must be honest when I say that change is NOT going to happen overnight. Do not let Satan deceive you into thinking that just because you begin to feel better about a situation or a person, that it is finished. Roots of bitterness can go deep, and the Lord wants them to die completely. A way to realize that change is taking place, is when presented with that person or memory; your emotions remain peaceful.

In the many years that have passed since this life-changing experience, I have found this godly principle to work in every difficult relationship. The key word is *work*! Just as the Israelites had to walk out their freedom through obedience, so will you. You and I have to learn how to trust

God's Word. This is the part of Christianity where I had failed in the past. I would give up much too soon, and would miss the blessing that God had for me. I highly recommend that you read as much as you can on the difference between body, soul and spirit. I Thessalonians 5:23 clearly reveals that God desires *that your whole spirit, soul, and body be kept blameless at the coming of our Lord Jesus Christ.* Andrew Wommack, author of *Spirit, Soul, and Body,* gives great insight into this mostly misunderstood part of our humanity.

I learned through each one of these circumstances how to start making the proper choices to believe God's Word and to receive by faith, in that Word, the desires of my heart. You can also.

Do not allow feelings to dominate you. You can change. As you practice focusing upon scriptures that contain the life-transforming power of God; they will cleanse and restore your soul.

E.W. Kenyon, author of *Signposts on the Road to Success*, wrote that our minds are tools that we must put to work. This wonderful instrument was created to be filled with the knowledge of God. When it has been ravaged by hurtful memories, it needs restoring. This takes time.

Mark 4:24 gives us another key to victory:

*Be careful what you are hearing. The MEASURE (of thought and study) YOU GIVE (to the truth you hear) will be the measure that COMES BACK to you, and more (besides) will be given to you who hear)* (Emphasis mine).

This is a timeless principle. We must guard our thoughts, as we journey onto freedom. As you work at *remembering* the right choice you have made to forgive, you will gain control over your thoughts.

James 1:4, *But let patience do a thorough work.* Be patient with yourself; God is.

*Forgive and Remember*

*Forgive and Remember*

# BUILDING YOUR MEMORIAL

Are you ready to begin your journey? Are you going to stay in the mud pits of Egypt when God has sent you a Savior Who is ready to lead you forth into victory? The choice truly is YOURS to make. Make that choice based on truth. Many of us read the testimonies of others. They thrill us for the moment and then end up on a shelf filled with the victory stories of others. Please do not let this book end up the same way.

Start writing your own victory story. This is the purpose of this book. I want to give you a brief synopsis on how to begin. I pray it will inspire you, and encourage you to learn, practice, and experience *forgive and remember.*

The tools you will need are simple:

1. An honest look at your current spiritual condition.
2. A humble heart to allow God's Word to teach you.
3. A small journal to keep a record of your journey.
4. A Bible.
5. Consistent time spent reading and studying.
6. A desire to sincerely forgive.

### *Forgive and Remember*

I learned a small, but valuable lesson many years ago. It was the practice of speaking out loud what I was going to do. For example, you begin by verbalizing, "I **WILL** learn how to forgive God's Way"! It is like pointing a flag in a certain direction. It is the freedom flag. Point it. Follow it.

God is with you on this journey. He knows what you need to set you on the path of *forgive and remember.* The stones placed at the Jordan River, after they crossed, were a memorial for the Israelites to **remember** God's faithfulness, protection, and provision. They heard His Word through Joshua, received it, and obeyed His instructions. Hear, receive, and obey. You may have to hear many times before it becomes a part of you, but trust me, it will be worth every moment you spend listening.

Difficult situations will always be a part of the human existence. Face that fact. However, the truth that promises God's Presence with us as He promised Joshua and Israelites is also fact. *He is the same yesterday, today and forever* (Hebrews 13:8).

There are a few important issues that need to be settled:

1. You cannot change your past.

2. You cannot change people.

3. You **can** change and be free.

God is not asking you to cover the hurt. What happened to you may have been horrendous. God did not want that for you. We live in a fallen world full of people who choose evil rather than good. He gave every human a free will, and in using that free will wrong choices are made, and people are hurt. God is here to help restore and heal the soul.

Your decision to learn this vital lesson can change your life forever as it did mine. As I stated earlier, I still use this plan and when worked diligently, it produces peace and joy. The greatest feeling you will have, is that day when you realize your thoughts and emotions are free from what has hurt you. Believe me ... it will come!

Let God give you the first memorial stone to look at daily. This stone will be His Word. Philippians 4:13, *I can do all things through Christ Who strengthens me.* Another wonderful scripture is Romans 8:38-39:

*For I am convinced that neither death nor life, neither angels nor demons, neither the present nor the future, nor any powers, neither height nor depth, nor anything else in all creation, will be able to separate us from the love of God that is in Christ Jesus our Lord.*

When you begin to understand the love God has for you, and His desire to see you made completely whole again, you will be on your way.

Let me summarize by offering you a definite plan:

1. Purchase a journal.

2. Write down who or what needs forgiveness.

3. Write your intent, "I will forgive and remember."

4. Write the date and time that you made your decision.

5. Inscribe these words, "I choose this day as an act of my will, and in obedience to God's Word to forgive _____, and their wrongs against me. From this moment on (date and time), I will REMEMBER that I have made the choice before God to forgive them. I will not take back those hurtful emotions to enslave me again. I commit these words of my heart to my Lord, and trust the Holy Spirit to keep me focused and determined. I will keep these words before my eyes, and will honor them before the Lord."

6. Next, write the offenses. Take them outside and burn them in a fire-safe container. As the fire consumes those evil actions, release forgiveness, and see the holy fire of God's grace consume them in your heart.

Now, the work begins. From this moment on, you will need to keep your journal and God's Word close to you because your emotions will fight you.

Whenever Satan tries to bring that hurtful memory back, state your purpose again, and refuse to accept his attack against you. The scripture in James 4:7 will help you, *"Submit yourselves to God, RESIST the devil, and he will flee."* Speak out and say, "Satan, I resist you in the Name of Jesus. I will not allow you to penetrate my thoughts. I have made my choice to forgive, and I remember my words of commitment to the Lord. Leave me, in Jesus Name!"

One of my favorite scriptures is Romans 8:37,

*Yet, amid all these things we are more than conquerors and gain a surpassing victory through Him Who loved us.*

The priests were in the midst of the mighty Jordan River, and stood on dry ground as the Israelites passed through to safety. Jesus, your Lord, stands with you in the midst of this time of obedience, and He will see you safely through to victory!!

2 Peter 1:3 states,

*For His divine power has bestowed upon us all things that (are requisite and suited) to life and godliness, through the (full, personal) knowledge of Him Who called us by and to His own glory and excellence (virtue).*

God's divine power is working in you. *He is the Guardian and Bishop of our souls* (I Peter 2:25).

God is with you. He knows the way to freedom. He is asking that you follow Him into the Jordan, pick up the stones in readiness to build your memorial of freedom and joy. He has made the way.

As you daily search His Word, hold to your commitment, and declare that your mind will be used to "remember" your righteous choices, your confession will be, "I have forgiven you and I will remember **this** choice."

God bless you as you journey to complete restoration and healing.

*Forgive and Remember*

*Forgive and Remember*

# RECEIVING JESUS AS SAVIOR

I want to take this opportunity to thank you for investing your time in the reading of my book. Someone may have given this to you, and you may desire to know more about becoming a Christian.

This is the most life changing decision that you will ever make. God loves you and desires above all things that you know His love personally. He is not interested in you becoming religious or spiritual. He wants you to have eternal life; His very life.

The Bible contains the truth of God's love. I would not have experienced the victory I have without Jesus Christ. Below, I want to share scriptures that I pray, will open the door of your heart to the Greatest Love you can ever know.

*God, our Savior...wants all men to be saved and to come to a knowledge of the truth.* (I Timothy 2:3-4)

*God, our Savior, saved us, not because of righteous things we had done, but because of His mercy. He saved us through the washing of rebirth and renewal by the Holy Spirit.* (Titus 3:5)

*If you confess with your mouth, "Jesus is Lord," and believe in your heart that God raised Him from the dead, you will be saved.* (Romans 10:9)

*In Jesus we have redemption through His blood, the forgiveness of sins, in accordance with the riches of God's grace.* (Ephesians 1:7)

God's grace (undeserved favor), has provided everything we need to be saved. He did it through His Son, Jesus Christ. Jesus personally bore our sins upon His body, and paid the price for our acceptance before God through His shed blood.

Salvation is a gift. It is to be received, because no one can earn it. If my words can help you take one step toward Jesus Christ; I rejoice. You have to take the step. God wants you to take it based on Truth, and not emotions. Jesus said, *"You will KNOW the Truth, and the Truth will make you free"* (John 8:32).

Ask God now to help you. Ask Him to lead you to the Truth. His Word is Truth. You may not "feel" worthy or sure of what you are doing. Believe me when I say God loves you. He died for you. He wants you to know the grace that paid the price for your eternal life.

Pray this prayer..."*God, I want to know You. Even though I do not understand everything now, I want to receive Jesus Christ as my Savior and Lord. I say with my own words that Jesus is Lord, and I choose to believe in my heart that You raised Him from the dead for me. Thank You for saving me. Thank You for leading me to greater understanding. I believe Jesus paid for my sins through the shedding of His blood, and that through faith in Him, I have become a child of God.*"

If you need further help, please email me at pastorchar59@yahoo.com. My prayer is that you will find a strong, Bible-believing church, where you can begin your new life, and continue to grow in the grace and knowledge of Jesus Christ.

*Forgive and Remember*

# Glossary of Terms

**Born Again**

to have a rebirth of the spirit. To enter into a personal relationship with Jesus Christ. To become a new creation in Christ Jesus.

**Godly**

One who is devout with a God-ward attitude, living a manner of life that reflects obedience to God's Word

**Grace**

The unmerited but freely given love of God towards men.

**Restore**

To bring back to a former or original condition. To bring back to health and vigor.

**Righteousness**

The character or quality of being right with God. It is being brought into a right relationship with God through Christ Jesus.

**Salvation**

Denotes deliverance and preservation granted immediately by God to those who accept His conditions of repentance and faith in the Lord Jesus Christ, Whose blood was shed for the payment of all sin.

**Soul**

The rational, volitional, and emotional faculties in man, forming an entity distinct from the body and the spirit.

**Transform**

To change the character, nature and condition of an individual by the power of God, through the intake of God's Word.

**Victim**

One who is killed, injured, or subjected to suffering by others.

## BIBLIOGRAPHY

Landorf, Joyce. *Irregular People*. 1982, Word Books,

Waco, Texas.

Kenyon, E.W. *Signposts on the Road to Success.* Kenyon's

Gospel Publishing Society, 1966

Wommack, Andrew. *Spirit, Soul, and Body.* Andrew

Wommack Ministries, Inc., 2005

*Forgive and Remember*

## NOTES

*Forgive and Remember*

84861012R00042

Made in the USA
San Bernardino, CA
13 August 2018